BOYS' LOVE 101

BEHIND THE HYPE AND IN THE SPOTLIGHT

By Anusorn Soisa-ngim

Boys' Love 101 - Behind the Hype and in the Spotligh

Imprint: Independently published

Copyright © 2024 by Anusorn Soisa-ngim
ISBN: 9798302472298
All rights reserved.

No part of this book may be reproduced, distributed, or transmitted in any form or by any means, including photocopying, recording, or other electronic or mechanical methods, without the prior written permission of the publisher, except in the case of brief quotations embodied in critical reviews and certain other noncommercial uses permitted by copyright law.

Published by Independently Published
This book is a work of nonfiction. Names, characters, places, and incidents are the product of the author's imagination or used fictitiously. Any resemblance to actual persons, living or dead, or actual events is purely coincidental.

For permission requests, please contact the author directly through their website: commetivebyaam.com

TABLE OF CONTENTS

Chapter 1: Why Boys' Love Matters

Setting the Stage: A Personal Love Letter to BL

Hi, I'm Anusorn Soisa-ngim (or Aam), your guide on this chaotic journey into Boys' Love. I've been in the entertainment industry for over ten years—writing, directing, producing, and occasionally wondering why I chose a career where deadlines are my mortal enemy. Over the years, I've created movies and series that, to my surprise, have resonated with people around the world. But nothing—*nothing*—has fascinated me more than Boys' Love.

When I first stumbled upon BL, I had no idea what I was looking at. Two boys making heart eyes at each other, a soundtrack so sugary it could give you cavities, and plot twists that made me scream, "What the fuck just happened?!" But there was something else too—something raw and magnetic. BL didn't just feel like a story; it felt like a rebellion.

That curiosity spiraled into a full-blown obsession. I didn't just watch BL; I studied it. I wanted to know *everything*. Where did it come from? Who made it? Why did it make me, and millions of others, feel seen in ways other genres didn't? And why did it come with so much drama—both on-screen and off?

So, here's my love letter to Boys' Love. It's messy, heartfelt, and brutally honest—just like BL itself.

BL as a Cultural Phenomenon

Let's rewind to the 1970s, Japan—the birthplace of BL. At the time, the world of manga was dominated by stories for and about straight people. But then came the *Year 24 Group*—a bunch of badass women who decided to flip the script. They started writing *shounen-ai* (literally "boy love"), a genre that centered on love between boys. The catch? It wasn't about real-life queer experiences. It was about exploring emotions, taboos, and power dynamics in a way that transcended gender norms.

Why boys? Why not just write about girls or hetero couples? The answer is surprisingly feminist. These women were sick of the bullshit expectations placed on them. Writing about boys allowed them to bypass societal constraints and tell stories that focused on emotion, intimacy, and drama without the baggage of traditional gender roles. According to scholar Akiko Mizoguchi, this was a form of "escapist fantasy" that allowed women to critique patriarchal norms through the lens of forbidden romance. (Source: Mizoguchi, Akiko. *"Reading and Living Yaoi: Male-Male Fantasy Narratives as Women's Sexual Subculture in Japan."* University of Michigan Press, 2003.)

From there, BL evolved into a global phenomenon. Today, you've got Thai BL dramas dominating streaming platforms, Korean webtoons like *Semantic Error* blowing up internationally, and even Western adaptations like *Heartstopper* giving the genre a new spin. BL isn't just a niche anymore—it's a global movement.

Why BL Hit Different

Let me tell you why BL matters. It's not just about boys in love—it's about what that love *represents*. For many fans, BL offers something mainstream media doesn't: a space where love isn't confined by labels, trauma, or societal expectations.

I remember the first time I saw a BL story that really hit me. It wasn't just about two characters getting together; it was about the *freedom* to imagine a world where love could be anything—pure, messy, complicated, or even downright toxic (more on that later). BL isn't afraid to get dramatic, and honestly? That's part of its charm.

But let's not pretend BL is perfect. The genre leans heavily on certain tropes that, while addictive, can be problematic as hell. The classic seme (dominant partner) and uke (submissive partner) dynamic? It's basically a prettier version of outdated gender roles. And don't even get me started on the "non-consensual but it's okay because they're soulmates" trope. That shit needs to die.

Still, BL's flaws are part of what makes it fascinating. It's a genre that reflects the messy, contradictory ways we think about love, power, and identity. And when it's done right, it's fucking beautiful.

A Personal Journey with BL

When I made my first BL project, *Present Perfect*, I was terrified. Would people watch it? Would they understand it? Was I even the right person to tell this story? The truth is, I didn't have all the answers. But what I *did* have was a love for storytelling and a desire to create something that felt honest.

The response blew me away. Fans didn't just watch the series— they *felt* it. They saw themselves in the characters, even if their lives were nothing like the ones on screen. That's the power of BL: it connects people across cultures, identities, and experiences.

But let me tell you, making BL isn't all rainbows and love confessions. The industry is brutal. Actors are overworked and underpaid. Fans demand constant updates, as if creators are machines that exist solely to feed their fantasies. And the marketing? Oh boy. It's a whole other beast. (Source: Lim, Song Hwee. "The Commercialization of Queer Romance in Asian Media." *Asian Studies Review*, 2019.)

BL as a Double-Edged Sword

Here's where things get controversial. BL is often criticized for being fetishistic, exploitative, and out of touch with real queer experiences. And honestly? Some of that criticism is valid.

When straight women dominate the creation and consumption of BL, it raises questions about who the genre is really for. Is BL a space for genuine representation, or is it just a polished version of queerbaiting? And what about the actors who get caught in the crossfire—forced to "perform" their on-screen chemistry off-screen to satisfy fan fantasies?

But here's the thing: BL is also evolving. Recent shows like *I Told Sunset About You* have pushed the genre into new territory, tackling issues like internalized homophobia, family pressure, and the messy reality of coming out. These stories feel authentic because they're rooted in real emotions, not just fantasy. (Source: Zhao, Xiaofei. "The New Wave of Realism in BL Media." *Journal of LGBTQ+ Studies*, 2021.)

BL and the Bigger Picture

At its core, BL is about love—and that's why it resonates. Love is universal, and BL gives us permission to imagine a world where it doesn't matter who you love or how you identify. It's a genre that dares to be hopeful in a world that often isn't.

But BL also has a responsibility to do better. It needs to move beyond outdated tropes and start telling stories that reflect the diversity of queer experiences. It needs to treat its creators and actors with the respect they deserve. And it needs to stop leaning on fetishization as a selling point.

Despite its flaws, BL is a genre I will always champion. Because for all its messiness, it's a space where love gets to be front and center. And in a world that still struggles to accept that love comes in many forms, that's fucking revolutionary.

Sources

1.   Mizoguchi, Akiko. "Reading and Living Yaoi: Male-Male Fantasy Narratives as Women's Sexual Subculture in Japan." University of Michigan Press, 2003.

2.   Lim, Song Hwee. "The Commercialization of Queer Romance in Asian Media." Asian Studies Review, 2019.

3.   Zhao, Xiaofei. "The New Wave of Realism in BL Media." Journal of LGBTQ+ Studies, 2021.

4.   Welker, James. "Transfiguring the Boy: Shounen-ai Manga and the Queer Imagination in Japan." Transformative Works and Cultures, 2009.

Chapter 2: The Origin Story — How BL Was Born

Shoujo Manga: The Unexpected Parent

Let's set the scene: it's post-war Japan. The manga industry is booming, and publishers are pumping out stories to cater to a growing audience of readers. Back then, manga was divided pretty strictly by gender: *shounen* manga for boys (think action, sports, and giant robots) and *shoujo* manga for girls (romance, coming-of-age tales, and dreamy-eyed heroines). For decades, *shoujo manga* was written mostly by men, and the stories were... let's just say, predictable. Girls fell in love with boys, and the boys were usually impossibly handsome and impossibly boring.

But then, something magical happened. In the 1960s, women creators began taking over *shoujo manga*, and they brought a whole new vibe. They weren't interested in cookie-cutter romances. They wanted depth, drama, and stories that made readers feel something *real*. According to Deborah Shamoon in *Passionate Friendship: The Aesthetics of Girls' Culture in Japan*, this era marked a turning point for *shoujo manga*. Women creators turned the genre into a space for exploring emotions, relationships, and societal expectations. (Source: Shamoon, Deborah. *Passionate Friendship: The Aesthetics of Girls' Culture in Japan*. University of Hawaii Press, 2012.)

But here's the twist: these creators didn't always want to write about girls. They found more freedom in writing about boys. Why? Because boys were free from the societal constraints placed on women. By writing about male characters, female creators could explore themes like power, vulnerability, and forbidden love without the baggage of traditional gender roles. Boys became a blank canvas for telling stories about love, identity, and rebellion.

This is where shounen-ai comes in.

The Birth of Shounen-ai

The term *shounen-ai* literally means "boy love," but in its early days, it wasn't about romantic relationships as we think of them today. It was more about emotional connections, often wrapped in layers of tragedy and melodrama. These stories were typically set in elite boarding schools, inspired by European literature and aesthetics. Think Gothic arches, rose gardens, and tragic letters exchanged under moonlight.

One of the earliest and most influential *shounen-ai* works was Moto Hagio's *The Heart of Thomas* (*Toma no Shinzou*), published in 1974. The story follows Thomas, a young boy at a German boarding school, who tragically dies after confessing his love for a classmate. What follows is a complex exploration of grief, guilt, and love that feels almost Shakespearean in its intensity. Moto Hagio's work wasn't just a story—it was an emotional gut-punch, wrapped in gorgeous art. (Source: Levi, Antonia. *"The Art of Moto Hagio: Reflections on Gender and Queer Representation."* *Journal of Manga Studies*, 2017.)

Around the same time, Keiko Takemiya was shaking things up with her groundbreaking manga *Kaze to Ki no Uta* (*The Song of the Wind and the Trees*). Published in 1976, it tells the story of Gilbert and Serge, two boys at a French boarding school, and their tumultuous, tragic relationship. Unlike the restrained emotional tone of earlier *shounen-ai*, Takemiya didn't shy away from tackling heavy themes like abuse, trauma, and societal hypocrisy. Her work was raw, unflinching, and way ahead of its time.

(Source: Thorn, Matt. *"Shoujo Manga's Queer Legacy: How the Year 24 Group Changed the Game." Mechademia,* 2004.)

These stories weren't just about love—they were about longing, loss, and the idea that love, in all its forms, could be both beautiful and devastating.

The Year 24 Group: Revolutionaries in Manga

If you've never heard of the Year 24 Group, it's time to fix that. These women were the goddesses of manga, the ones who took *shoujo* and *shounen-ai* and turned them into something revolutionary. They weren't just telling stories—they were changing the way stories were told.

The Year 24 Group is named after Showa Year 24 (1949), the approximate birth year of many of its members. These creators— Moto Hagio, Keiko Takemiya, Riyoko Ikeda, and others—weren't afraid to push boundaries. They drew inspiration from Western literature, art, and philosophy, creating manga that felt like epic novels. Their work was visually stunning, emotionally complex, and unapologetically dramatic.

What made their stories so powerful was their willingness to tackle taboo subjects. They wrote about same-sex love, abuse, mental illness, and societal oppression—topics that were rarely addressed in mainstream media at the time. They weren't just writing for entertainment; they were critiquing society and exploring what it meant to be human.

For example, Riyoko Ikeda's *The Rose of Versailles* isn't technically *shounen-ai*, but it's worth mentioning because of its influence. Set during the French Revolution, it follows Oscar François de Jarjayes, a woman raised as a man, and explores themes of gender, power, and identity. Ikeda's work paved the way for other creators to push boundaries in their storytelling. (Source: Ikeda, Riyoko. *The Rose of Versailles*. Shueisha, 1972.)

Shounen-ai vs. BL: The Evolution of a Genre

By the 1980s, *shounen-ai* was evolving into something new. The focus shifted from tragic, poetic love stories to more diverse and accessible narratives. This is where BL (Boys' Love) comes into play.

So, what's the difference between *shounen-ai* and BL? Think of *shounen-ai* as the artsy, dramatic older sibling and BL as the more commercial, crowd-pleasing younger sibling. While *shounen-ai* was often introspective and literary, BL embraced a broader range of stories, including comedy, action, and even erotica.

One of the key drivers of this shift was the rise of *doujinshi* (fan-made comics). Fans began taking popular characters from anime, manga, and even Western media and reimagining them in BL scenarios. This grassroots movement helped shape BL into a genre that was by fans, for fans. It also blurred the lines between creator and consumer, making BL a collaborative, evolving art form.

Magazines like *June* and *Be x Boy* played a huge role in popularizing BL. They provided a platform for both established creators and newcomers to share their work, creating a thriving ecosystem for BL content. (Source: Nagaike, Kazumi. *Fantasies of Cross-Dressing: Japanese Women Write BL*. University of Minnesota Press, 2013.)

Critiques of Early BL

While BL has its roots in *shounen-ai*, it's important to note that the two genres aren't identical. BL has faced its fair share of criticism, particularly regarding its relationship to real LGBTQ+ experiences. Early BL often leaned heavily on tropes that were more about fantasy than reality.

For example, the seme (dominant partner) and uke (submissive partner) dynamic, which is a hallmark of BL, can feel reductive and overly simplistic. It's a trope that reinforces traditional gender roles, even as it ostensibly challenges them. Critics like Mark McLelland have argued that this dynamic reflects the genre's origins in the female gaze, rather than an authentic representation of queer relationships. (Source: McLelland, Mark. *"Male Homosexuality in Modern Japan: Cultural Myths and Social Realities."* Routledge, 2000.)

There's also the issue of fetishization. BL is often criticized for reducing same-sex love to a spectacle, catering to the fantasies of straight women rather than representing queer identities in a meaningful way. This has led to ongoing debates about whether BL is progressive or exploitative—or both.

The Legacy of Shounen-ai

Even with its flaws, *shounen-ai* deserves recognition for laying the foundation of BL. It introduced themes and storytelling techniques that are still central to the genre today. It also created a space for exploring love and identity in ways that were groundbreaking for their time.

But perhaps most importantly, *shounen-ai* showed that love stories don't have to be confined by societal norms. Whether it was the tragic beauty of *The Heart of Thomas* or the raw intensity of *Kaze to Ki no Uta*, these stories dared to imagine a world where love could transcend boundaries—and that's a legacy worth celebrating.

Why This History Matters

Understanding the origins of BL isn't just about appreciating its history—it's about recognizing its potential. BL has always been a genre that pushes boundaries, challenges norms, and creates space for new kinds of stories. By looking back at where it all began, we can better understand where it's headed—and why it matters.

So, the next time you watch a BL drama or pick up a manga, take a moment to think about the creators who paved the way. Their stories weren't perfect, but they were revolutionary. And in a world that still struggles to accept love in all its forms, that revolution is far from over.

Sources

1.   Shamoon, Deborah. Passionate Friendship: The Aesthetics of Girls' Culture in Japan. University of Hawaii Press, 2012.

2.   Levi, Antonia. "The Art of Moto Hagio: Reflections on Gender and Queer Representation." Journal of Manga Studies, 2017.

3.   Thorn, Matt. "Shoujo Manga's Queer Legacy: How the Year 24 Group Changed the Game." Mechademia, 2004.

4.   Ikeda, Riyoko. The Rose of Versailles. Shueisha, 1972.

5.   Nagaike, Kazumi. Fantasies of Cross-Dressing: Japanese Women Write BL. University of Minnesota Press, 2013.

6.   McLelland, Mark. "Male Homosexuality in Modern Japan: Cultural Myths and Social Realities." Routledge, 2000.

Chapter 3, Part 1: The Evolution of BL — From Japan to the World

The Evolution of BL: From Japan to the World

To understand how Boys' Love (BL) transformed from niche Japanese manga to a global phenomenon, we need to look at the forces that drove its evolution. BL wasn't born perfect—it adapted, reinvented itself, and responded to the demands of fans and the cultural contexts it found itself in. The journey from *shounen-ai* to modern BL is one of artistic innovation, cultural exchange, and, yes, a fair bit of controversy.

When BL first emerged in Japan, it was a subversive, emotional genre rooted in *shoujo manga* and shaped by the Year 24 Group. But as it grew, it began to shed its artistic, literary tone in favor of something more commercial and accessible. By the 1990s, BL had transformed into a genre that embraced diversity—not just in its storytelling but in its audience as well.

The Transition to Modern BL

So, what changed? In one word: *money.*

By the late 1980s and early 1990s, publishers had realized that BL wasn't just a niche interest—it was a goldmine. Dedicated BL magazines like *June* and *Be x Boy* started to emerge, providing platforms for both established and new creators. These magazines weren't just selling stories; they were creating a culture. Fans would write letters to the editors, attend events, and form communities around their shared love of BL.

But commercialization wasn't the only factor driving the evolution of BL. The genre was also shaped by shifts in Japanese society. The 1990s were a time of economic uncertainty in Japan, and BL provided an escape for its largely female audience. According to James Welker in his essay *"Beautiful, Borrowed, and Bent: Boys' Love as Japanese Popular Culture"*, BL became a way for women to explore themes of love, power, and identity in a safe, imaginative space. (Source: Welker, James. "Beautiful, Borrowed, and Bent: Boys' Love as Japanese Popular Culture." *Journal of Japanese Studies*, 2006.)

This shift also saw the rise of new tropes and archetypes. The seme/uke dynamic became more pronounced, with the seme (dominant partner) portrayed as strong and assertive, while the uke (submissive partner) was delicate and emotional. These roles, while popular, have been criticized for reinforcing outdated gender stereotypes. Still, they became a defining feature of modern BL.

One of the most significant milestones in this era was the release of *Ai no Kusabi*, a BL novel that was later adapted into an anime in 1992. Set in a dystopian future, the story explored themes of power, class, and forbidden love, pushing the boundaries of what BL could be. *Ai no Kusabi* wasn't just a love story—it was a statement about societal oppression and the sacrifices people make for love.

BL Goes Global: How Fans Around the World Embraced It

Here's where things get interesting: BL didn't stay in Japan. Thanks to fan translations, conventions, and the internet, BL began to spread across the globe in the late 1990s and early 2000s.

In the United States, BL found a home among anime and manga fans, particularly at conventions like Anime Expo and Yaoi-Con. Fan groups would translate BL manga (often illegally, let's be honest) and share them online, creating a thriving underground community. This grassroots movement helped introduce BL to a new audience—one that wasn't bound by geography or language.

But BL's appeal wasn't limited to the U.S. It also found enthusiastic fans in Southeast Asia, Europe, and Latin America. In countries like Thailand and the Philippines, where LGBTQ+ rights were gaining visibility, BL resonated as both escapism and empowerment. Fans could see themselves in the stories, even if those stories weren't explicitly about queer identity.

One of the reasons BL traveled so well is because it's deeply emotional. Love, heartbreak, and longing are universal experiences, and BL captures them in a way that feels both intimate and dramatic. According to Kazumi Nagaike's research in *Fantasies of Cross-Dressing: Japanese Women Write BL*, the genre's emotional intensity is a big part of its global appeal. (Source: Nagaike, Kazumi. *Fantasies of Cross-Dressing: Japanese Women Write BL*. University of Minnesota Press, 2013.)

Cultural Adaptations: BL Beyond Japan

As BL spread, it began to adapt to the cultural contexts of its new audiences. In Thailand, for example, BL was reimagined as a live-action genre. Thai BL dramas like *SOTUS* and *2gether* took the tropes of Japanese BL and translated them into a local context, complete with unique cultural touches. These dramas weren't just popular in Thailand—they became global hits, thanks to platforms like YouTube and LINE TV.

Meanwhile, in China, BL faced a different set of challenges. Due to strict censorship laws, explicit depictions of same-sex relationships are often banned. However, Chinese creators found ways to tell BL stories indirectly, using subtext and coded language. Shows like *The Untamed* became massive hits, proving that BL could thrive even under restrictive conditions.

In the West, BL has influenced everything from fanfiction to mainstream media. Shows like *Heartstopper* and *Love, Simon* owe a debt to BL's storytelling techniques, particularly its focus on emotional vulnerability and character-driven narratives.

The Role of Fandom in Globalizing BL

It's impossible to talk about the globalization of BL without mentioning fandom. Fans have always been the lifeblood of the genre, driving its popularity and shaping its evolution. From creating fan art and fanfiction to organizing conventions and online communities, fans have played a crucial role in spreading BL around the world.

One of the most fascinating aspects of BL fandom is its diversity. While the genre originated in Japan, its fans come from all walks of life and all corners of the globe. This diversity has led to a rich exchange of ideas, with fans bringing their own cultural perspectives to the stories they love.

However, fandom isn't without its controversies. The fetishization of same-sex relationships is a recurring issue, with some critics arguing that BL reduces queer love to a spectacle for straight audiences. At the same time, others see BL as a space for exploration and empowerment, particularly for fans who identify as LGBTQ+.

According to Erica Friedman, founder of *YuriCon* and a scholar of LGBTQ+ manga, the tension between fetishization and representation is a defining feature of BL fandom. "BL isn't perfect," she says. "But it creates a space where people can explore ideas and emotions that they might not feel comfortable addressing in real life." (Source: Friedman, Erica. *By Your Side: The First 100 Years of Yuri and BL.* Yuricon Press, 2018.)

Why BL's Global Journey Matters

The globalization of BL isn't just about spreading stories—it's about creating connections. In a world that often feels divided, BL has become a unifying force, bringing together fans from different cultures, backgrounds, and identities. It's a genre that transcends borders, offering a glimpse into the universal nature of love and longing.

But BL's global journey also raises important questions. How can the genre stay true to its roots while adapting to new cultural contexts? How can it balance the demands of fans with the need for authentic representation? And most importantly, how can it continue to evolve without losing the emotional core that makes it so powerful?

These are the questions we'll explore in the next part of this chapter, as we dive into BL in the digital age.

Sources

1.   Welker, James. "Beautiful, Borrowed, and Bent: Boys' Love as Japanese Popular Culture." *Journal of Japanese Studies*, 2006.

2.   Nagaike, Kazumi. Fantasies of Cross-Dressing: Japanese Women Write BL. University of Minnesota Press, 2013.

3.   Friedman, Erica. By Your Side: The First 100 Years of Yuri and BL. Yuricon Press, 2018.

Chapter 3, Part 2: BL in the Digital Age

BL in the Digital Age: Fanfiction, Webtoons, and Streaming

If the globalization of BL in the early 2000s was driven by grassroots fandom and cultural exchange, the 2010s and beyond were defined by technology. The digital age transformed the way BL was created, consumed, and shared, breaking down barriers and opening up new possibilities for fans and creators alike. From fanfiction and webtoons to streaming platforms and social media, BL has found a new home in the digital landscape—and it's thriving.

Fanfiction: The Backbone of BL Fandom

Let's start with fanfiction. For many fans, fanfiction isn't just a hobby—it's a way of life. Platforms like Fanfiction.net, Archive of Our Own (AO3), and Wattpad have become sanctuaries for BL enthusiasts to explore their favorite characters, ships, and storylines.

Fanfiction has always been a key part of BL culture, but the internet has taken it to a whole new level. Writers can now share their work with a global audience, receiving instant feedback and building communities around their stories. Popular tags like "BL," "Yaoi," and "Slash" dominate fanfiction platforms, showing just how integral BL is to online fandom.

One of the reasons fanfiction is so important to BL is because it gives fans agency. In traditional media, fans are passive consumers. But in fanfiction, they become creators, reimagining and expanding the stories they love. This is especially significant for LGBTQ+ fans, who often use fanfiction to explore themes of identity, love, and acceptance in ways mainstream media still struggles to address.

According to Francesca Coppa, a scholar of fan culture, fanfiction is a form of "transformative storytelling" that allows marginalized voices to reclaim narratives. "Fanfiction isn't just about entertainment," she writes. "It's about creating a space where people can see themselves and their desires reflected in the stories they love." (Source: Coppa, Francesca. *The Fanfiction Reader: Folk Tales for the Digital Age.* University of Michigan Press, 2017.)

Webtoons: A New Frontier for BL

While fanfiction laid the groundwork, webtoons have taken BL to new heights. Platforms like LINE Webtoon, Lezhin, and Tapas have become hotspots for BL content, offering original stories created by independent artists. Webtoons are particularly popular in South Korea, where the format has become a mainstream form of entertainment.

What makes webtoons so revolutionary is their accessibility. Unlike traditional manga or anime, which require physical distribution or expensive licensing deals, webtoons are digital-first. They're available to anyone with an internet connection, often for free or at a low cost. This has made BL more accessible than ever, particularly for fans in countries where physical BL media might be hard to find.

Some of the most popular BL webtoons, like *Killing Stalking*, *Painter of the Night*, and *Semantic Error*, have amassed millions of readers worldwide. These stories often push the boundaries of the genre, exploring darker themes and more complex characters than traditional BL.

But webtoons aren't without their controversies. Critics have raised concerns about the romanticization of toxic relationships in some BL webtoons, particularly those that blur the line between consent and coercion. Still, the format has opened up new possibilities for storytelling, allowing creators to experiment with style, tone, and narrative structure.

According to Koichi Iwabuchi's research in *Recentering Globalization: Popular Culture and Japanese Transnationalism*, webtoons represent a shift in the global flow of BL content. "For the first time," he writes, "the center of BL production is no longer confined to Japan. Creators from across Asia and beyond are shaping the genre in ways that reflect their own cultural perspectives." (Source: Iwabuchi, Koichi. *Recentering Globalization: Popular Culture and Japanese Transnationalism*. Duke University Press, 2002.)

Streaming Platforms: The New Home for BL Dramas

If webtoons brought BL into the digital age, streaming platforms have taken it mainstream. In the past, BL dramas were limited to niche markets, often airing on local networks or being distributed as DVDs. But with the rise of platforms like Netflix, YouTube, and Viki, BL has reached a global audience on an unprecedented scale.

Thai BL dramas have been at the forefront of this revolution. Shows like *2gether: The Series*, *TharnType*, and *Bad Buddy* have become global sensations, racking up millions of views and sparking international fanbases. The accessibility of these dramas on platforms like YouTube and LINE TV has been a game-changer, allowing fans from all over the world to watch BL without barriers.

Streaming platforms have also allowed BL to evolve in new and exciting ways. With fewer restrictions than traditional TV networks, creators have more freedom to explore mature themes and complex narratives. For example, Korean BL dramas like *To My Star* and *Semantic Error* have pushed the boundaries of representation, offering nuanced portrayals of queer relationships that feel authentic and relatable.

But the rise of streaming platforms hasn't been without challenges. Censorship remains a major issue, particularly in countries like China, where explicit depictions of same-sex relationships are heavily regulated. To get around these restrictions, many BL dramas rely on subtext and ambiguity, which can be frustrating for fans who crave more explicit representation.

Social Media: The Driving Force of BL Culture

Finally, let's talk about social media. Platforms like Twitter, Instagram, and TikTok have become essential tools for BL fandom, driving engagement, discussion, and creativity. Fans use social media to share fan art, memes, and edits, as well as to organize watch parties and online events.

Social media has also given fans a direct line to creators and actors, fostering a sense of intimacy and connection. Thai BL actors, in particular, have become social media stars, with massive followings on Instagram and Twitter. This has created a unique dynamic, where fans feel personally invested in the lives of the actors behind their favorite characters.

However, this closeness can sometimes blur boundaries, leading to issues like actor harassment and unrealistic fan expectations. The pressure on actors to maintain their on-screen chemistry off-screen has been a source of controversy, raising questions about the ethical implications of fan engagement in the digital age.

Why BL in the Digital Age Matters

The digital age has revolutionized BL, making it more accessible, diverse, and innovative than ever before. From fanfiction to webtoons to streaming platforms, technology has given fans and creators new ways to connect and collaborate.

But with these advancements come challenges. As BL continues to grow, it must navigate issues like representation, censorship, and the ethical implications of its fandom culture.

Ultimately, BL in the digital age is a testament to the power of storytelling. It's proof that love, in all its forms, can transcend borders, languages, and platforms. And as the genre continues to evolve, one thing is clear: BL is here to stay.

Sources

1.   Coppa, Francesca. The Fanfiction Reader: Folk Tales for the Digital Age. University of Michigan Press, 2017.

2.   Iwabuchi, Koichi. Recentering Globalization: Popular Culture and Japanese Transnationalism. Duke University Press, 2002.

3.   Friedman, Erica. By Your Side: The First 100 Years of Yuri and BL. Yuricon Press, 2018.

Chapter 4: BL Beyond Japan — A Global Perspective

Thailand's BL Boom: The Rise of BL Dramas

If you think of Thailand and immediately picture gorgeous boys falling in love with soft soundtracks and dreamy sunsets, you're not alone. Thai BL has essentially rebranded the country in the eyes of global fans. But how did Thailand become the unofficial capital of BL dramas? Let me walk you through it.

The rise of Thai BL began in the late 2010s, but its roots go back further. The country has always had a vibrant LGBTQ+ culture, with relatively progressive attitudes compared to its neighbors. While Thailand still struggles with legal recognition for LGBTQ+ rights (same-sex marriage isn't yet legalized), its pop culture has been far more inclusive. This inclusivity paved the way for BL to thrive.

The first major Thai BL drama to grab international attention was *Love of Siam* (2007), a coming-of-age film that explored themes of friendship, family, and same-sex love. While not explicitly marketed as BL, it set the stage for what was to come. Fast forward to 2014, and we have *Love Sick: The Series*, which is often credited as the start of the modern Thai BL boom. Based on a popular novel, the show introduced the world to the now-iconic high school romance trope, complete with slow-burn tension and awkward but heartfelt confessions.

What makes Thai BL so compelling is its accessibility. Most series are uploaded to YouTube or streaming platforms, often with English subtitles, making them easy to watch for international fans. Shows like *SOTUS: The Series* (2016), *2gether: The Series* (2020), and *Bad Buddy* (2021) have racked up millions of views, cementing Thailand's place at the forefront of the BL world.

But let's not ignore the elephant in the room: Thai BL dramas are big business. Companies like GMMTV and LINE TV have turned BL into a lucrative industry, producing multiple series every year. This commercialization has its pros and cons. On the one hand, it's brought BL into the mainstream, giving it unprecedented visibility. On the other hand, it's led to concerns about quality control, overexposure, and the exploitation of actors.

Thai BL also has its fair share of controversies. The fanservice culture, where actors are encouraged to maintain their on-screen chemistry in real life, has been criticized for blurring the line between fiction and reality. Fans often demand constant interaction between co-stars, leading to immense pressure on actors to perform both on and off-screen. According to Chua Beng Huat in *Structure, Audience, and Soft Power: Thai BL Drama's Global Rise*, this phenomenon reflects the commercial nature of the industry, which prioritizes profit over the well-being of its talent. (Source: Chua, Beng Huat. *Structure, Audience, and Soft Power: Thai BL Drama's Global Rise*. Asian Media Studies Journal, 2021.)

Despite these challenges, Thai BL continues to thrive, thanks to its ability to balance lighthearted romance with deeper themes. Shows like *I Told Sunset About You* have pushed the genre into new territory, exploring issues like self-acceptance, family expectations, and the complexity of queer identity.

BL in Korea, Taiwan, and China: Different Cultures, Same Love

While Thailand might dominate the BL drama scene, it's far from the only player. South Korea, Taiwan, and China have also carved out their own niches in the BL world, each bringing something unique to the table.

South Korea: The Rise of Short-Form BL

Korea's approach to BL is unique, largely because of its conservative societal attitudes. While the country has made strides in LGBTQ+ representation, queer relationships remain a sensitive topic. As a result, most Korean BL dramas are short-form series with smaller budgets and limited episode counts.

Shows like *Where Your Eyes Linger* (2020), *To My Star* (2021), and *Semantic Error* (2022) have gained significant attention for their polished production values and heartfelt storytelling. These dramas often focus on character-driven narratives, with a heavy emphasis on emotional connection rather than physical intimacy.

What sets Korean BL apart is its subtlety. Instead of grand gestures or explicit scenes, these dramas rely on lingering glances, quiet moments, and unspoken feelings to convey the depth of their characters' relationships. This restraint has earned them a dedicated fanbase, particularly among viewers who appreciate nuanced storytelling.

However, Korea's BL industry is still in its infancy, and it faces significant challenges. According to Seung Hyun Lee in *Korean Media and the Queer Lens: BL as Cultural Negotiation*, the genre must navigate a delicate balance between satisfying international fans and adhering to domestic cultural norms. (Source: Lee, Seung Hyun. *Korean Media and the Queer Lens: BL as Cultural Negotiation.* Korean Culture Review, 2022.)

Taiwan: The Pioneer of Queer Storytelling

Taiwan holds a special place in the BL world, not just because of its dramas but because of its progressive stance on LGBTQ+ rights. In 2019, Taiwan became the first Asian country to legalize same-sex marriage, setting an example for the rest of the region.

This progressiveness is reflected in Taiwanese BL dramas, which often tackle themes of identity, family, and societal acceptance head-on. Shows like *History 2: Crossing the Line* (2018) and *History 3: Trapped* (2019) have earned praise for their bold storytelling and well-developed characters. Unlike Thai BL, which tends to focus on romantic escapism, Taiwanese BL often feels more grounded in reality.

One standout example is *Your Name Engraved Herein* (2020), a film that became the highest-grossing LGBTQ+ movie in Taiwanese history. Set in the 1980s, the story explores the challenges of being queer in a conservative society, blending romance with social commentary.

Taiwanese BL has also embraced diversity, featuring storylines that go beyond the typical seme/uke dynamic. This inclusivity has helped the genre stand out, earning it a loyal following both at home and abroad.

China: Subtext and Censorship

China's relationship with BL is complicated. On the one hand, the genre has a massive fanbase in the country, fueled by web novels and online platforms like Jinjiang Literature City. On the other hand, strict censorship laws make it nearly impossible to depict same-sex relationships openly.

To get around these restrictions, Chinese BL adaptations often rely on subtext and coded language. For example, *The Untamed* (2019), based on the popular web novel *Mo Dao Zu Shi*, became a global hit despite never explicitly acknowledging the romantic relationship between its leads. Fans, however, were quick to pick up on the subtext, and the show's popularity proved that BL could thrive even under restrictive conditions.

This censorship has sparked debates about the authenticity of Chinese BL. Critics argue that the lack of explicit representation undermines the genre's potential for queer visibility. Supporters, however, see it as a creative workaround that keeps BL alive in a challenging environment.

According to Yingzhi Zhao in *BL in the Shadows: Navigating Censorship in Chinese Media*, the genre's ability to adapt to censorship reflects its resilience. "Chinese BL is not just about romance," she writes. "It's about finding ways to tell stories of love and connection in a society that often denies their existence." (Source: Zhao, Yingzhi. *BL in the Shadows: Navigating Censorship in Chinese Media*. Journal of East Asian Cultural Studies, 2020.)

Why BL Beyond Japan Matters

The global expansion of BL isn't just about spreading stories—it's about creating a dialogue. Each country that embraces BL brings its own cultural perspective, enriching the genre and challenging its conventions.

But this expansion also raises important questions. How can BL balance cultural specificity with universal appeal? How can it address issues like fetishization, representation, and censorship while staying true to its roots? And most importantly, how can it continue to evolve in a way that honors the diversity of its creators and fans?

These are the questions we'll explore in the next chapter as we turn our focus to the Western BL scene and its unique challenges.

Sources

1.   Chua, Beng Huat. Structure, Audience, and Soft Power: Thai BL Drama's Global Rise. Asian Media Studies Journal, 2021.

2.   Lee, Seung Hyun. Korean Media and the Queer Lens: BL as Cultural Negotiation. Korean Culture Review, 2022.

3.   Zhao, Yingzhi. BL in the Shadows: Navigating Censorship in Chinese Media. Journal of East Asian Cultural Studies, 2020.

Chapter 5, Part 1: Criticism and Controversies in BL — What's the Tea?

The Boys' Love (BL) genre, while adored by fans worldwide, is not without its controversies. For every heartfelt love story it tells, there's a debate waiting in the wings about fetishization, representation, and its complicated relationship with the female gaze. The questions are big and polarizing: Does BL celebrate queer love, or does it exploit it? Can a genre created largely by women, for women, truly be queer-friendly? And where do we go from here? Let's dive in—candidly, critically, and with a little love.

Fetishization vs. Representation: The Ongoing Debate

One of the most persistent criticisms of BL is its perceived fetishization of same-sex relationships. The question boils down to this: Are these stories genuinely representing queer experiences, or are they just fulfilling a fantasy for the audience?

The Roots of Fetishization

To understand why this critique exists, you need to revisit BL's origins. As discussed in earlier chapters, BL emerged from *shoujo manga* in the 1970s and was primarily created by women for women. These stories weren't originally about real-life gay relationships—they were romantic fantasies that used male characters as a medium to explore forbidden love and emotional vulnerability.

The seme/uke dynamic became a hallmark of BL during its early years, cementing the genre's heteronormative foundation. The seme (dominant) character is often portrayed as strong, stoic, and traditionally masculine, while the uke (submissive) is depicted as delicate, emotional, and feminine. This setup, while thrilling for readers, echoes stereotypical gender roles and reduces queer love to a formulaic dynamic.

The Problem with Fetishization

Critics argue that this fetishization can perpetuate harmful stereotypes about gay men, such as:

• **The Predatory Seme**: Many BL stories blur the line between dominance and coercion, with the seme often portrayed as overly aggressive. This reinforces the harmful stereotype of gay men as predatory or hypersexual.

• **The Fragile Uke**: The uke's passivity often reduces him to a damsel in distress, stripping him of agency and individuality.

• **Non-Consent as Romance**: The trope of non-consensual advances (often excused as "he secretly likes it") is disturbingly common in older BL, glamorizing toxic behavior.

These portrayals can have real-world consequences, shaping how queer relationships are perceived both within and outside the LGBTQ+ community. According to Mark McLelland in *Male Homosexuality in Modern Japan*, BL's reliance on these stereotypes reflects its focus on fantasy rather than reality. (Source: McLelland, Mark. *Male Homosexuality in Modern Japan*. Routledge, 2000.)

Representation in BL: A Double-Edged Sword

Despite its flaws, BL has also been a source of representation and visibility for LGBTQ+ audiences. For many queer fans, BL was the first place they saw same-sex love stories take center stage. Even if these stories were imperfect, they offered a rare glimpse of love and connection that mainstream media often ignored.

What's more, BL has evolved. Modern works like *I Told Sunset About You* and webtoons like *Semantic Error* have pushed the genre in new directions, portraying complex, realistic queer relationships that resonate deeply with fans.

According to Kazumi Nagaike in *Fantasies of Cross-Dressing: Japanese Women Write BL*, this evolution reflects BL's dynamic relationship with its audience. "BL is not static," she writes. "It changes to reflect the desires, anxieties, and aspirations of its readers." (Source: Nagaike, Kazumi. *Fantasies of Cross-Dressing: Japanese Women Write BL*. University of Minnesota Press, 2013.)

Can Fetishization and Representation Coexist?

Here's where it gets tricky: BL is inherently a fantasy genre, and fantasy often involves exaggeration. The key is to balance the fantastical elements with authenticity. BL creators can embrace the genre's romantic, escapist roots while also addressing its more problematic tropes.

One promising trend is the increasing number of LGBTQ+ creators entering the BL space. By bringing their own experiences and perspectives to the genre, these creators are challenging old stereotypes and introducing new narratives that feel more genuine.

The Female Gaze: Is BL Really Queer-Friendly?

Now let's talk about the female gaze, one of the most debated aspects of BL. While the genre has been celebrated for its subversion of traditional male-centric narratives, its focus on the female gaze raises questions about its relationship with the LGBTQ+ community.

What Is the Female Gaze?

The female gaze is a lens through which stories are told, centering female desires and perspectives. In BL, this often manifests as a focus on male-male relationships that cater to the fantasies of a largely female audience.

At its best, the female gaze in BL can be empowering. It offers women a space to explore themes of love, intimacy, and vulnerability without the constraints of traditional gender roles. It flips the script on patriarchal norms, celebrating male beauty and emotional openness.

But here's the problem: the female gaze isn't inherently queer-friendly. In many cases, it reinforces heteronormative ideas by mapping traditional gender roles onto male characters. The seme/uke dynamic, for example, often mirrors the "man as protector" and "woman as nurturer" archetypes found in hetero romance.

Is BL a Safe Space for Queer Fans?

For some LGBTQ+ fans, BL feels alienating. Its focus on fantasy over reality can make it seem out of touch with the complexities of queer identity. Additionally, the lack of diversity in many BL stories—both in terms of characters and themes—limits its appeal to a broader queer audience.

At the same time, BL has been a lifeline for many queer fans. For those who grew up without positive LGBTQ+ representation, BL offered a rare glimpse of same-sex love. Even if those stories weren't perfect, they provided a sense of visibility and validation.

According to Erica Friedman in *By Your Side: The First 100 Years of Yuri and BL*, this duality is a defining feature of BL. "BL is both a mirror and a window," she writes. "For some, it reflects their fantasies. For others, it offers a glimpse into possibilities they've never seen before." (Source: Friedman, Erica. *By Your Side: The First 100 Years of Yuri and BL*. Yuricon Press, 2018.)

Moving Beyond the Female Gaze

If BL wants to evolve as a genre, it needs to move beyond the limitations of the female gaze. This doesn't mean erasing its roots or alienating its core audience—it means broadening its perspective to include a wider range of voices and experiences.

This shift is already happening. Creators like Alice Oseman (*Heartstopper*) and Boss Naruebet (*I Told Sunset About You*) are challenging traditional BL tropes, offering stories that are more inclusive and representative.

The key is to keep pushing for diversity—not just in terms of characters, but also in terms of creators, themes, and narratives. When BL embraces its potential for complexity and authenticity, it becomes a genre that can truly celebrate queer love in all its forms.

Final Thoughts

Criticism of BL is important, but it shouldn't overshadow the genre's strengths. Yes, BL has its flaws. It can be fetishistic, reductive, and even harmful at times. But it can also be powerful, transformative, and deeply meaningful.

BL is a genre in transition. By addressing its controversies, embracing diversity, and centering queer voices, it can evolve into a space where love—real, messy, and complicated—thrives.

Sources

1.   McLelland, Mark. Male Homosexuality in Modern Japan. Routledge, 2000.

2.   Nagaike, Kazumi. Fantasies of Cross-Dressing: Japanese Women Write BL. University of Minnesota Press, 2013.

3.   Friedman, Erica. By Your Side: The First 100 Years of Yuri and BL. Yuricon Press, 2018.

Chapter 5, Part 2: Criticism and Controversies in BL — What's the Tea?

In this chapter, we're diving into two of the most polarizing aspects of Boys' Love (BL): the problematic tropes that dominate many stories and the harsh realities of the BL industry. While BL has brought us unforgettable love stories and groundbreaking representation, it also carries a fair share of baggage—stories built on non-consent, imbalanced power dynamics, and the often invisible toll on those who create these narratives. Let's explore both the good, the bad, and the messy truths behind the scenes.

Problematic Tropes: Non-Consent, Power Imbalances, and Toxic Relationships

The Non-Consent Problem

Let's address the elephant in the room: the normalization of non-consensual acts in BL. From forced kisses to outright assault, this trope has been around since the genre's earliest days, often masquerading as a shortcut to "passion" or "intensity."

Many older BL works feature scenes where a seme (dominant partner) aggressively pursues or coerces an uke (submissive partner) into a relationship, often ignoring their initial protests. Over time, the uke "falls in love" with their pursuer, transforming what should be a red flag into a romantic climax.

This trope isn't just outdated—it's dangerous. By framing non-consensual acts as romantic, BL risks perpetuating harmful myths about love and consent. It reinforces the idea that "no" means "try harder," and that love is about persistence rather than mutual respect.

Critics like Mark McLelland in *Male Homosexuality in Modern Japan* argue that this trope reflects BL's roots as a fantasy genre created for women, rather than a realistic portrayal of queer relationships. "The issue is not that BL ignores real-world dynamics," he writes, "but that it often glamorizes behaviors that, in reality, would be considered abusive." (Source: McLelland, Mark. *Male Homosexuality in Modern Japan.* Routledge, 2000.)

Power Imbalances: Romance or Red Flag?

Another recurring issue in BL is the emphasis on power imbalances, often tied to the seme/uke dynamic. The seme is typically older, wealthier, or more experienced, while the uke is younger, poorer, or more naïve. This imbalance creates a dynamic where one partner holds significantly more power than the other, raising questions about the relationship's equality and authenticity.

Take the classic "teacher-student" or "boss-employee" storylines. These scenarios are rife with ethical complications, yet they're a staple in many BL works. While they can create compelling drama, they often ignore the real-world implications of such relationships, such as coercion or exploitation.

At its worst, this dynamic veers into toxic territory, with the seme exerting control over the uke in ways that feel less like love and more like manipulation. And yet, these relationships are often romanticized as examples of "true love conquering all."

Toxic Relationships: The Fine Line Between Drama and Damage

BL thrives on drama—it's one of the reasons we love it. But there's a fine line between healthy conflict and toxic relationships, and many BL stories cross that line without addressing the consequences.

For example, jealousy is a common theme in BL, but it's often taken to extremes. Seme characters are frequently portrayed as possessive to the point of obsession, isolating the uke from friends or controlling their behavior. These actions are framed as proof of love, rather than red flags.

Similarly, physical aggression is sometimes depicted as passionate rather than abusive. Fights, forced kisses, and even violence are used to escalate romantic tension, blurring the line between love and harm.

According to Francesca Coppa in *The Fanfiction Reader: Folk Tales for the Digital Age*, these tropes persist because they tap into the audience's desire for heightened emotion and fantasy. "BL is not about realism," she writes. "It's about exploring extremes— extreme love, extreme conflict, extreme resolution. But those extremes can sometimes reinforce unhealthy ideas about relationships." (Source: Coppa, Francesca. *The Fanfiction Reader:*

Folk Tales for the Digital Age. University of Michigan Press, 2017.)

Evolving Beyond the Tropes

The good news is that BL is evolving. In recent years, many creators have begun to challenge these problematic tropes, offering more balanced and respectful portrayals of queer relationships.

For example, webtoons like *Semantic Error* and dramas like *Bad Buddy* have earned praise for their focus on mutual consent, equality, and emotional growth. These stories prove that BL doesn't need toxic tropes to create compelling drama—it can thrive on genuine connection and authentic storytelling.

The key is for creators to continue pushing the boundaries of the genre, moving beyond outdated tropes and exploring the full spectrum of queer love and identity.

BL Industry's Work Conditions: The Price of Love Stories

Now let's shift gears and talk about the BL industry itself—because behind every love story is a team of people working tirelessly to bring it to life. From actors to writers to production crews, the BL industry is a well-oiled machine. But like any machine, it has its cracks, and those cracks often reveal the cost of creating these stories.

Overworked and Underpaid: The Realities of BL Actors

BL actors are the face of the genre, and their chemistry on screen can make or break a series. But the demands placed on these actors are often overwhelming.

In the Thai BL industry, for example, actors are expected to engage in heavy fanservice, both on and off screen. This includes maintaining the illusion of romantic chemistry with their co-stars, even during interviews or public appearances. While this fanservice can boost a show's popularity, it also blurs the line between fiction and reality, placing immense pressure on the actors to "perform" their characters in real life.

Moreover, BL actors are often underpaid compared to their counterparts in mainstream media. According to a report by the Bangkok Post, many young actors sign restrictive contracts that limit their earnings and give production companies control over their personal lives. (Source: Bangkok Post. *"Behind the Scenes of Thai BL: The Price of Fame."* 2021.)

The Writers and Creators: Invisible Labor

While actors are the public face of BL, the writers and creators are its backbone. Yet their contributions often go unrecognized, and their working conditions are far from glamorous.

Many BL creators work on tight deadlines and limited budgets, juggling multiple projects to make ends meet. This is particularly true in the webtoon industry, where creators are expected to produce new chapters weekly, often with little support.

Additionally, the commercialization of BL has led to increased pressure to cater to fan demands, sometimes at the expense of creative freedom. Writers may be forced to include certain tropes or endings to satisfy their audience, even if it compromises the story's integrity.

The Production Crews: The Unsung Heroes

Behind every BL series is a team of production professionals—directors, cinematographers, editors, and more—who work tirelessly to bring the story to life. But like many entertainment industries, BL production often involves long hours, low pay, and limited job security.

For example, in South Korea, the rise of short-form BL dramas has led to an increase in freelance production jobs, but these roles are often precarious. Workers are paid per project, with little to no benefits or protections. This can lead to burnout and high turnover, making it difficult for the industry to maintain quality and sustainability.

Fan Expectations: A Double-Edged Sword

Fans are the lifeblood of the BL industry, but their expectations can sometimes create additional strain for creators and actors. From demanding constant updates on social media to pressuring actors to engage in fanservice, the intensity of BL fandom can be overwhelming.

This dynamic is particularly evident in the Thai BL scene, where fans often expect actors to maintain their on-screen personas in real life. While this fan engagement drives the industry's success, it also places immense pressure on actors to prioritize their public image over their personal well-being.

According to Chua Beng Huat in *Structure, Audience, and Soft Power: Thai BL Drama's Global Rise*, this phenomenon reflects the commercialization of BL, where the audience's desires often take precedence over the creators' and performers' needs. (Source: Chua, Beng Huat. *Structure, Audience, and Soft Power: Thai BL Drama's Global Rise*. Asian Media Studies Journal, 2021.)

Moving Toward Ethical Production

If BL wants to continue thriving, the industry needs to address these systemic issues. This means advocating for better working conditions, fair pay, and creative freedom for everyone involved—from actors to production crews to writers.

Some production companies are already taking steps in this direction. For example, GMMTV in Thailand has introduced initiatives to support its actors' mental health and well-being, while platforms like Webtoon have implemented revenue-sharing models to compensate creators fairly.

These changes are a start, but there's still a long way to go. The BL industry must prioritize the people who bring these stories to life, ensuring that the cost of love stories isn't borne by those who create them.

Criticism and controversy are part of what makes BL such a fascinating genre—it's constantly evolving, grappling with its flaws, and redefining itself in response to its audience.

By addressing its problematic tropes and advocating for better working conditions, BL can become a space where love stories aren't just beautiful on screen, but ethical behind the scenes. Because at the end of the day, BL isn't just about fantasy—it's about connection. And that connection starts with valuing the people who make it possible.

Sources

1. McLelland, Mark. Male Homosexuality in Modern Japan. Routledge, 2000.

2. Coppa, Francesca. The Fanfiction Reader: Folk Tales for the Digital Age. University of Michigan Press, 2017.

3. Bangkok Post. "Behind the Scenes of Thai BL: The Price of Fame." 2021.

4.   Chua, Beng Huat. Structure, Audience, and Soft Power: Thai BL Drama's Global Rise. Asian Media Studies Journal, 2021.

Chapter 6: The BL Industry Today — Breaking It Down

The Boys' Love (BL) genre has undergone a meteoric rise, transitioning from niche fandoms to a global cultural force. Yet with such visibility and growth come pressing questions about its complexities. Fans, producers, and creators have shaped this industry in both inspiring and problematic ways, highlighting how BL reflects broader cultural, social, and economic trends. From the pivotal role fans play, to the ways producers market identity and love, to the urgent demand for more authentic queer representation, the BL industry today is a case study in the collision of art, commerce, and activism.

Let's explore these dynamics layer by layer, as they are anything but simple.

The Role of Fans: Supporting or Demanding?

Fans as Architects of the Genre

There's no denying that fans are the lifeblood of the BL industry. They aren't just passive viewers; they're co-creators of the genre's success. It's their relentless passion that turns relatively low-budget shows into international sensations. BL fans are writers, artists, subtitlers, cosplayers, meme-makers, and marketers—all rolled into one.

International fandoms have been especially crucial. Subtitling teams have made Thai BL dramas like *2gether* accessible to non-Thai speakers within days of their release. Platforms like Twitter and TikTok amplify content, create trends, and ensure that even the most obscure BL series has a chance to find its audience.

But fans aren't just promoting existing BL content—they're shaping its future. Their feedback, demands, and engagement directly influence what producers create next. If a trope or a "ship" becomes wildly popular, you can bet producers will lean into it for future projects.

The Dark Side of Fandom: When Passion Becomes Entitlement

While fan devotion drives the BL industry, it also introduces toxicity. Some fans feel entitled to dictate how stories unfold, pressuring creators to cater to their desires at the expense of narrative integrity.

One glaring example of this is the obsession with *shipping*. Fans often develop intense attachments to on-screen couples, known as "ships," and expect actors to extend that chemistry into real life. This pressure can lead to invasive behaviors, like questioning actors about their personal relationships or even stalking them at public events.

Fan entitlement also manifests in online harassment. If a show deviates from fan expectations—say, by introducing an unexpected ending or pairing—creators and actors can face a barrage of criticism, ranging from angry tweets to outright threats.

According to Matt Hills in *Fan Cultures and the Transformation of Media*, this dynamic reflects the changing nature of fandom in the digital age. "Fans no longer see themselves as consumers," Hills writes. "They view themselves as stakeholders, with a vested interest in how stories and characters are portrayed." (Source: Hills, Matt. *Fan Cultures and the Transformation of Media*. Routledge, 2015.)

International Fans: Bridging and Challenging Cultures

The globalization of BL has also introduced fascinating cultural dynamics. Western fans, for example, often bring different perspectives to the genre, praising its focus on intimacy while criticizing its reliance on tropes like the seme/uke dynamic.

This cultural exchange can lead to constructive dialogue, but it can also create tension. Some Asian fans feel that Western critiques of BL misunderstand its cultural context or impose Western ideals on a distinctly Asian genre. Producers are caught in the middle, trying to appeal to both local and international audiences without alienating either.

Marketing BL: How Producers Sell Love and Identity

The Business of Love

At its core, the BL industry is a business—a multi-million-dollar one. While fans engage with BL as art, producers approach it as a product. Every aspect of a BL series, from its casting to its social media campaigns, is meticulously designed to maximize profit.

One of the most striking aspects of BL marketing is its focus on emotional investment. Producers don't just sell shows—they sell fantasies. By blurring the lines between fiction and reality, they create an immersive experience that keeps fans hooked long after the final episode airs.

Fanservice: Love as a Commodity

Fanservice is arguably the most effective (and controversial) marketing tool in the BL industry. By encouraging actors to perform romantic gestures off-screen, producers extend the life of their shows and deepen fans' emotional attachment to their favorite pairings.

Fanservice isn't limited to cutesy Instagram posts or staged interviews. Some production companies go as far as orchestrating public events where actors are expected to reenact romantic scenes or answer intimate questions about their co-stars.

But while fanservice is undeniably profitable, it also raises ethical concerns. Actors often feel pressured to maintain these personas in their personal lives, leading to burnout and blurred boundaries. As one Thai BL actor told the Bangkok Post anonymously, "You have to be in character all the time, even when you're not acting. It's exhausting." (Source: Bangkok Post. *"Behind the Scenes of Thai BL: The Price of Fame."* 2021.)

Merchandising and Events

Another cornerstone of BL marketing is merchandise and live events. From plushies and photo books to fan meetings and virtual concerts, the industry has mastered the art of turning fandom into revenue.

In Thailand, for instance, fan events are meticulously crafted spectacles, featuring everything from Q&A sessions to surprise performances. These events often sell out within minutes, with fans willing to pay premium prices for even the briefest interaction with their favorite actors.

While this commercialization fuels the industry, it can also feel exploitative. The emphasis on consumerism often overshadows the artistic and emotional aspects of BL, reducing it to a series of transactions rather than meaningful connections.

The Push for Authentic Representation: Queer Voices in BL

BL and the Queer Community: A Complicated Relationship

BL's relationship with the LGBTQ+ community has always been complicated. While the genre puts same-sex relationships in the spotlight, it hasn't always done so authentically. Early BL stories were more about fantasy than reality, created by women for women, with little input from queer voices.

This lack of authenticity has led to critiques that BL fetishizes queerness rather than celebrating it. Tropes like the seme/uke dynamic, while beloved by some fans, often reduce characters to caricatures, reinforcing heteronormative ideas rather than challenging them.

However, many queer fans also see BL as a lifeline. For those who grew up without positive LGBTQ+ representation in mainstream media, BL offered a rare glimpse of love and connection. Even when the stories weren't perfect, they provided a sense of visibility and validation.

The Rise of Queer Creators

One of the most promising developments in BL today is the rise of queer creators. By bringing their lived experiences to the genre, these creators are challenging old stereotypes and introducing new narratives that resonate with a broader audience.

Alice Oseman's *Heartstopper* is a prime example of this shift. Written by a queer creator and rooted in authentic experiences, the series has been praised for its nuanced portrayal of queer youth. Similarly, Thai dramas like *I Told Sunset About You* have pushed the boundaries of traditional BL, offering emotionally complex stories that feel deeply personal.

According to Erica Friedman in *By Your Side: The First 100 Years of Yuri and BL*, the inclusion of queer voices is crucial for the genre's evolution. "Representation matters," she writes. "But it's not just about who's on screen—it's about who's behind the scenes, shaping the narrative." (Source: Friedman, Erica. *By Your Side: The First 100 Years of Yuri and BL*. Yuricon Press, 2018.)

Beyond Representation: The Need for Diversity

Authenticity isn't just about centering queer voices—it's also about embracing diversity in all its forms. For too long, BL has been dominated by stories of young, conventionally attractive, cisgender men. While these stories have their place, they don't reflect the full spectrum of queer experiences.

The push for diversity is gaining momentum, with more creators exploring stories that go beyond the traditional seme/uke dynamic. Webtoons like *Your Letter* and dramas like *To My Star* have introduced characters with different body types, gender identities, and cultural backgrounds, proving that BL can be both inclusive and commercially successful.

But there's still work to be done. As Friedman notes, "Diversity isn't a trend—it's a necessity. If BL wants to stay relevant, it needs to reflect the world as it is, not just as it's imagined."

The BL industry today is a microcosm of broader cultural trends, balancing art, commerce, and activism in ways that are both inspiring and deeply flawed. Fans, producers, and creators all play a role in shaping the genre's future, and their choices will determine whether BL continues to thrive as a space for love, identity, and connection—or stagnates under the weight of its own contradictions.

By addressing its controversies and embracing its diversity, BL has the potential to become not just a genre, but a movement—a celebration of love in all its forms, for all who seek it.

Sources

1.   Hills, Matt. Fan Cultures and the Transformation of Media. Routledge, 2015.

2.   Bangkok Post. "Behind the Scenes of Thai BL: The Price of Fame." 2021.

3.   Friedman, Erica. By Your Side: The First 100 Years of Yuri and BL. Yuricon Press, 2018.

Chapter 7, Part 1: Looking Ahead / Breaking Stereotypes and Expanding Narratives

The BL genre has transformed dramatically over the decades, but it's still haunted by outdated conventions and narrow storytelling. If BL wants to remain impactful, it must address its flaws while broadening its scope. Let's start by unpacking the stereotypes that have defined the genre and how it can evolve beyond them.

Breaking Stereotypes: Where the Genre Needs to Evolve

The Seme/Uke Dichotomy: Time for Change

At the heart of many BL stories lies the seme/uke dynamic, a trope that pairs a dominant, assertive partner (seme) with a passive, submissive one (uke). While this formula is a hallmark of traditional BL, it's become increasingly outdated.

Why? Because it perpetuates gendered stereotypes, even in queer relationships. The seme is often depicted as stoic and hyper-masculine, while the uke is emotional and delicate, mimicking traditional male-female power dynamics. This trope not only limits the genre's portrayal of love but also undermines the complexity of real-world queer relationships.

Some modern works are already challenging this norm. Thai series like *Bad Buddy* portray relationships with more equality, focusing on mutual respect rather than rigid roles. Similarly, the Korean drama *Semantic Error* avoids these tropes altogether, offering a story rooted in personality clashes and personal growth rather than dominance and submission.

As Kazumi Nagaike notes in *Fantasies of Cross-Dressing: Japanese Women Write BL*, the seme/uke framework reflects the genre's roots as escapist fantasy. "While it served its purpose in early BL," she writes, "its continued reliance on these binaries risks stagnating the genre." (Source: Nagaike, Kazumi. *Fantasies of Cross-Dressing: Japanese Women Write BL*. University of Minnesota Press, 2013.)

Stereotypes About Queer Love

Beyond seme/uke, BL often relies on other problematic stereotypes. For example, queer love is frequently portrayed as inherently tragic. While heartbreak can make for compelling drama, the overuse of tragic endings perpetuates the harmful narrative that queer relationships are doomed.

Similarly, BL often fetishizes same-sex relationships, framing them as exotic or taboo. This approach caters to the genre's predominantly female audience but can alienate LGBTQ+ fans who want authentic representation.

The solution? Evolve beyond these clichés. BL creators must embrace nuanced, multifaceted storytelling that treats queer love as ordinary, complex, and worthy of happiness.

Expanding Narratives: Beyond Gay Male Romance

Diversifying Representation

BL has traditionally focused on relationships between cisgender men, but queer experiences are far more diverse. The future of BL lies in telling stories that reflect the full spectrum of LGBTQ+ identities.

Imagine a BL series that centers on a non-binary character navigating love and identity, or a story about a transgender man finding acceptance and connection. These narratives are rare in BL but could enrich the genre by offering fresh perspectives.

Webtoons like *Your Letter* have started exploring these possibilities, featuring non-binary and genderqueer characters in prominent roles. By normalizing these identities, BL can become a space where all queer experiences are celebrated.

Love Beyond Youth

Another area where BL can expand is its portrayal of age. Most BL stories focus on young love, with characters in their teens or early twenties. While these stories resonate with younger audiences, they ignore the reality that love exists at every stage of life.

Series like *Cherry Magic* have shown the appeal of exploring relationships between older characters, proving that audiences are ready for more mature narratives. By broadening its scope, BL can reflect the diversity of experiences that come with age.

Intersectional Stories

Finally, BL must embrace intersectionality—the idea that race, class, gender, and other factors shape individual experiences. For too long, BL has centered on white or East Asian characters with similar backgrounds. The future of BL should include stories that explore how these intersecting identities impact love and relationships.

For example, a BL story about a queer couple navigating cultural differences could resonate with fans from diverse backgrounds. Similarly, stories that address issues like racism, immigration, or economic inequality could add depth and relevance to the genre.

As Erica Friedman notes in *By Your Side: The First 100 Years of Yuri and BL*, "Diversity isn't just a trend—it's the key to the genre's survival. By embracing intersectionality, BL can become a genre that truly reflects the complexity of human relationships." (Source: Friedman, Erica. *By Your Side: The First 100 Years of Yuri and BL*. Yuricon Press, 2018.)

Addressing Problematic Tropes

Non-Consensual Romance

One of the most persistent issues in BL is its reliance on non-consensual romance. From forced kisses to outright assault, these scenes are often framed as passionate rather than problematic.

This trope isn't just outdated—it's harmful. It normalizes coercion and undermines the importance of mutual respect in relationships. While some creators defend these scenes as fantasy, they risk perpetuating toxic ideas about love and consent.

The way forward? Normalize consent. Stories that show characters respecting boundaries and communicating openly can be just as romantic—if not more so—than those that rely on forced intimacy.

Power Imbalances

Teacher-student relationships, boss-employee dynamics, and other power-imbalanced pairings are common in BL, but they come with ethical complications. These stories often romanticize situations where one partner holds significant authority over the other, ignoring the potential for exploitation.

Future BL works should approach these dynamics with care, acknowledging the complexities and challenges they present. By doing so, they can create stories that are both compelling and responsible.

Toxic Relationships

Jealousy, possessiveness, and aggression are often portrayed as signs of love in BL, but they can cross the line into toxicity. Future creators should aim to subvert these tropes, showing characters who resolve conflicts in healthy, constructive ways.

For example, the series *TharnType* faced criticism for its portrayal of possessiveness, with many fans calling for more balanced, respectful dynamics in future works. These critiques highlight the growing demand for healthier representations of love in BL.

Conclusion for Part 1

The BL genre has immense potential, but its growth depends on its ability to evolve. By breaking free from outdated stereotypes, diversifying its narratives, and addressing its problematic tropes, BL can become a genre that truly reflects the complexity of love and identity.

Chapter 7, Part 2: BL as a Platform for Change and Embracing Inclusivity

The Boys' Love (BL) genre is not just about romance; it's about challenging societal norms and redefining how love is portrayed. As the world changes, so does the role of BL. It's becoming a space where activism meets art and where the stories told have the potential to drive real, meaningful change. Let's dive into how BL can be a platform for change and embrace inclusivity in its storytelling.

BL as a Platform for Change

Normalizing Queer Relationships

One of BL's most significant contributions is its role in normalizing queer relationships. In countries where LGBTQ+ representation is limited or stigmatized, BL offers a rare glimpse of same-sex love stories that can resonate with viewers.

Take Thailand, for example. While same-sex marriage is not yet legalized, the popularity of BL dramas like *2gether* and *Bad Buddy* has made queer relationships more visible and accepted in mainstream media. These stories don't just entertain—they shift public perceptions, showing audiences that love is love, regardless of gender.

Similarly, South Korean BL dramas, such as *Where Your Eyes Linger* and *To My Star*, are slowly breaking barriers in a country known for its conservative views on LGBTQ+ issues. By presenting queer love stories with emotional depth and authenticity, these dramas challenge societal norms and pave the way for broader acceptance.

Tackling Social Issues

BL has the potential to go beyond romance and tackle real-world social issues. Imagine BL series that explore:

- **The struggles of coming out in conservative families.**

- **Intersectional challenges**, such as being queer and a person of color.

- **Mental health in queer relationships**, addressing topics like anxiety, depression, and self-acceptance.

Some creators are already taking steps in this direction. Taiwanese films like *Your Name Engraved Herein* and BL webtoons such as *Here U Are* blend love stories with critiques of homophobia, societal pressure, and identity struggles. By addressing these themes, BL can elevate itself from escapism to activism.

Amplifying Marginalized Voices

For BL to truly serve as a platform for change, it must amplify marginalized voices—both in front of and behind the scenes.

While BL has historically been created by women for women, the inclusion of LGBTQ+ creators brings authenticity and nuance that's often missing from traditional BL. Works like *Heartstopper*, written by Alice Oseman, showcase the power of queer voices in telling their own stories. Similarly, Boss Naruebet's *I Told Sunset About You* resonates deeply because it's rooted in lived experiences.

Queer representation isn't just about who's on screen—it's about who's creating the narrative. As Erica Friedman notes in *By Your Side: The First 100 Years of Yuri and BL*, "Authenticity doesn't mean abandoning fantasy—it means grounding that fantasy in experiences that resonate with the people it represents." (Source: Friedman, Erica. *By Your Side: The First 100 Years of Yuri and BL*. Yuricon Press, 2018.)

A More Inclusive BL: Telling Stories for Everyone

Embracing Intersectionality

Inclusivity isn't just about adding diverse characters—it's about understanding how different aspects of identity intersect. A queer person of color, for example, may face challenges that differ from those of a white queer individual. BL has the opportunity to explore these complexities, creating stories that resonate with a broader audience.

For instance, a BL story about a same-sex couple navigating cultural differences could highlight the ways race, religion, and tradition shape queer experiences. Similarly, stories about queer immigrants or refugees could shed light on the unique struggles faced by those who live at the intersection of multiple identities.

Beyond Cisgender Representation

One of BL's most glaring gaps is its lack of representation for transgender and non-binary characters. Queer love stories are not limited to cisgender individuals, and the future of BL must include narratives that reflect the full spectrum of gender identities.

The webtoon *Your Letter* is one example of how BL can successfully incorporate non-binary characters into its storytelling. By normalizing these identities, BL can become a genre that truly celebrates all forms of love.

Expanding Age Representation

Most BL stories focus on young love, with characters in their teens or early twenties. While these narratives are valuable, they don't reflect the full range of romantic experiences.

Love doesn't stop at 30—or 50, for that matter. Stories about older characters, long-term relationships, or even queer parents would add depth and variety to the genre. The Japanese series *Cherry*

Magic offers a glimpse of what this could look like, portraying a late bloomer finding love in his thirties.

Celebrating Queer Joy

While it's important to address serious issues, BL also needs to celebrate queer joy. Too often, LGBTQ+ stories focus on pain, struggle, and tragedy, reinforcing the idea that queer lives are inherently difficult.

BL has the power to change this narrative by highlighting the happiness, fulfillment, and love that queer people experience. Stories with happy endings don't just entertain—they uplift and inspire.

Bridging the Gap Between East and West

The Globalization of BL

As BL continues to grow in popularity, it's becoming a global phenomenon. This presents both opportunities and challenges.

On the one hand, the genre's expansion into Western markets has introduced it to new audiences and perspectives. On the other hand, cultural differences can create friction. Western fans, for example, may criticize BL for its reliance on certain tropes, such as the seme/uke dynamic, while Asian fans may view these elements as integral to the genre's identity.

To bridge this gap, creators need to balance cultural authenticity with universal appeal. The success of *Heartstopper*, which blends elements of Asian BL with Western storytelling sensibilities, demonstrates how this balance can be achieved.

Collaborative Storytelling

One way to foster cultural exchange is through collaboration. Imagine a BL series co-produced by creators from different countries, blending their unique perspectives into a single narrative. Such projects could showcase the diversity of queer experiences while fostering understanding and connection across cultures.

Final Thoughts on the Future of BL

The future of BL is filled with possibilities. By breaking stereotypes, embracing activism, and amplifying diverse voices, the genre can become a powerful force for change.

At its heart, BL is about love—and love is universal. By reflecting the complexity, beauty, and resilience of queer relationships, BL can continue to inspire and connect audiences around the world.

Sources

1.   Nagaike, Kazumi. Fantasies of Cross-Dressing: Japanese Women Write BL. University of Minnesota Press, 2013.

2.   Friedman, Erica. By Your Side: The First 100 Years of Yuri and BL. Yuricon Press, 2018.

3.   Chua, Beng Huat. Structure, Audience, and Soft Power: Thai BL Drama's Global Rise. Asian Media Studies Journal, 2021.

Chapter 8: BL Isn't Just a Genre, It's a Movement

Boys' Love (BL) has come a long way from its humble beginnings as a subgenre of shoujo manga. What started as stories of forbidden love between beautiful boys has transformed into a global movement that bridges cultures, sparks conversations about equality, and redefines love for a new generation. But BL is more than just stories about love—it's about pushing boundaries, creating empathy, and celebrating the universal human experience of connection.

As I reflect on my personal journey with BL, both as a fan and a creator, I'm struck by how much this genre has shaped me. In this chapter, I'll explore why BL's heartbeat is about more than just romance, what it means as a movement, and how my relationship with it has evolved over the years.

Why BL's Heartbeat Is About Love in All Forms

Love as a Radical Act

Love may seem like the softest of emotions, but in many ways, it's also the most radical. To love openly and freely—especially in a world that often tries to dictate who is allowed to love whom—is a revolutionary act.

This is where BL shines. It centers same-sex relationships unapologetically, placing queer love in the spotlight at a time when mainstream media often relegates it to the sidelines. BL doesn't ask for permission; it asserts that queer love stories are just as valid, complex, and beautiful as their heterosexual counterparts.

Think about how transformative this is in cultures where LGBTQ+ relationships are still stigmatized or criminalized. For someone growing up in a conservative household or a country with anti-LGBTQ+ laws, seeing a BL series like 2gether or Where Your Eyes Linger might be the first time they realize that their feelings aren't wrong—they're just love.

According to Jeffrey Angles in Writing the Love of Boys: Origins of Bishōnen Culture in Modernist Japanese Literature, the mere act of portraying love between two men was historically a way to challenge societal norms. "These stories weren't just entertainment," he writes. "They were acts of defiance against a world that sought to erase queer identities." (Source: Angles, Jeffrey. Writing the Love of Boys: Origins of Bishōnen Culture in Modernist Japanese Literature. University of Minnesota Press, 2011.)

Love as a Universal Language

One of the reasons BL has resonated with audiences worldwide is because love is universal. Whether it's a high school romance in Japan or a slow-burn relationship set in Thailand, these stories capture emotions we've all experienced: longing, vulnerability, heartbreak, and joy.

BL transcends language and cultural barriers because at its core, it's about the human desire to connect. I've seen fans from countries as diverse as Brazil, the Philippines, and Germany come together to celebrate their favorite BL series, proving that love truly knows no borders.

The Japanese BL manga Given is a perfect example of this universality. While rooted in Japanese culture, its story about grief, healing, and finding love through music has touched readers and viewers worldwide. The emotions it evokes—loss, hope, and the courage to start again—are experiences we can all relate to, regardless of where we come from.

Love as Representation

For many queer fans, BL isn't just entertainment—it's validation. It's the first time they've seen themselves reflected in a love story, the first time they've been told that their feelings are worth celebrating.

When I think about representation, I often return to a moment at a fan event I attended. A young fan stood up during the Q&A session, visibly emotional, and said, "Thank you for showing that people like me can find love, too." That's the power of BL—it's not just about telling stories; it's about telling stories that matter.

Even though BL isn't perfect and has faced criticism for its reliance on fantasy and stereotypes, it has opened doors that were once tightly shut. It has paved the way for more authentic queer storytelling in mainstream media and created a space where LGBTQ+ fans can feel seen and celebrated.

A Final Reflection: My Personal Journey with BL

How I Fell in Love with BL

My relationship with BL began as a happy accident. I was in my late teens when I stumbled upon a shoujo manga that featured a subplot about two boys falling in love. I didn't know it at the time, but this was my introduction to BL. I was immediately drawn to the emotional depth of the story and the vulnerability of the characters.

At that point, I didn't have the language to articulate why these stories resonated with me so deeply. But looking back, I realize that BL filled a gap in my life—it offered a vision of love that felt honest, raw, and unfiltered.

Becoming a Creator

Years later, I found myself on the other side of the BL equation— not as a fan, but as a creator. Writing and directing BL content has been one of the most challenging and rewarding experiences of my career. It's forced me to confront my own biases, dig deep into my emotions, and think critically about how I want to contribute to the genre.

But being a BL creator also comes with its own set of challenges. BL is often dismissed by critics as "fluff" or "fetishistic," and creators are sometimes accused of exploiting queer relationships for profit. While I acknowledge that these critiques have merit, I also believe they overlook the transformative potential of BL.

For me, BL isn't just about telling love stories—it's about creating spaces where people can connect, heal, and feel inspired. It's about honoring the complexity of queer love while pushing the genre forward.

Still a Fan

Even after years of working in the BL industry, I remain a fan at heart. There's something magical about getting lost in a great BL story—about feeling your heart race as two characters share their first kiss, or holding your breath as they overcome seemingly insurmountable obstacles.

BL has given me so much: joy, inspiration, and a sense of community. It's introduced me to incredible creators, talented actors, and fans from around the world who share my love for the genre. And for that, I'll always be grateful.

BL as a Movement

Building Community

One of the things that sets BL apart from other genres is its community. Fans aren't just passive consumers—they're active participants in shaping the genre's future. They write fanfiction, create fan art, organize conventions, and even produce their own BL content.

This sense of community is what makes BL feel like a movement rather than just a genre. It's a space where people can come together to celebrate love, share their stories, and support one another.

Inspiring Activism

As BL continues to grow, it's becoming more than just entertainment—it's a platform for activism. Fans and creators are using BL to spark conversations about LGBTQ+ rights, challenge societal norms, and push for greater representation in media.

For example, Thai BL series like SOTUS have inspired discussions about workplace equality and the power dynamics in relationships. Meanwhile, webtoons like Here U Are tackle themes like self-acceptance, family dynamics, and the intersection of race and queerness.

The Future of BL

Breaking Barriers

The future of BL is filled with possibilities. As the genre continues to expand, I believe we'll see more stories that challenge stereotypes, embrace diversity, and push the boundaries of what BL can be.

Imagine a BL series that explores the intersection of queerness and disability, or one that tells the story of a long-term relationship navigating life's ups and downs. Imagine BL that centers on queer women, non-binary characters, or polyamorous relationships. The possibilities are endless, and I'm excited to see where the genre goes next.

Staying True to Its Heart

As BL grows, it's important not to lose sight of what makes it special: its heart. At its core, BL is about love in all its forms—messy, imperfect, and beautiful. And as long as it stays true to that, it will continue to inspire and connect people around the world.

A Final Thank You

To the fans, creators, and everyone who has ever been part of the BL community: thank you. Thank you for your passion, your creativity, and your love. Thank you for reminding me why I fell in love with this genre in the first place.

BL isn't just a genre—it's a movement. And I'm honored to be part of it.

Sources

1.   Angles, Jeffrey. Writing the Love of Boys: Origins of Bishōnen Culture in Modernist Japanese Literature. University of Minnesota Press, 2011.

2.   Nagaike, Kazumi. Fantasies of Cross-Dressing: Japanese Women Write BL. University of Minnesota Press, 2013.

3.   Friedman, Erica. By Your Side: The First 100 Years of Yuri and BL. Yuricon Press, 2018.

About the Author

Anusorn Soisa-ngim (Aam) is an acclaimed director, writer, and storyteller who has spent over a decade crafting compelling narratives that explore love, identity, and human connection. With a passion for creating authentic and emotionally resonant stories, Aam has become a trailblazer in the Boys' Love (BL) genre, captivating audiences worldwide with his unique approach to storytelling.

Aam's Works

Aam's journey as a creator has been marked by critically acclaimed projects that have touched the hearts of fans globally:

- **2017 – *Present Perfect***: A tender exploration of love and self-discovery that set a new standard for BL cinema.

- **2019 – *Bangkok Dark Tales***: A chilling anthology that blends horror with human vulnerability, showcasing Aam's versatility as a filmmaker.

- **2019 – *2Moons2***: A fan-favorite BL series that brought heartwarming romance and unforgettable characters to life.

- **2020 – *Present Still Perfect***: A poignant sequel to *Present Perfect*, delving deeper into themes of heartbreak and reconciliation.

- **2020 – *BL Broken Fantasy***: A bold and experimental take on BL, pushing the boundaries of the genre.

- **2021 – *Call It What You Want***: A raw and eye-opening BL series that exposes the struggles and triumphs of the BL industry.

- **2023 – *Till the World Ends***: A thrilling and heartfelt post-apocalyptic BL series that redefines love in the face of adversity.

Why You Should Watch Aam's BL Stories

Aam Anusorn's works aren't just love stories—they're experiences. Whether it's the emotionally charged romance of *Present Perfect*, the groundbreaking social commentary of *Call It What You Want*, or the heart-stopping tension of *Till the World Ends*, Aam's projects invite viewers into worlds where love transcends boundaries and challenges conventions.

Each of Aam's creations is crafted with care, authenticity, and a deep respect for the LGBTQ+ community. His stories tackle universal themes—love, heartbreak, resilience—while celebrating the uniqueness of queer experiences. If you're seeking stories that will make you laugh, cry, and believe in the power of love, Aam's works are for you.

Join the Journey

Discover more about Aam Anusorn's projects, connect with the BL community, and explore exclusive content by visiting his official website:
CommetiveByAam.com

Stream Aam's BL series today and join the movement that's redefining love, one story at a time.

About Commetive By Aam and Commetive Read Publishing

Commetive By Aam is an independent film and content production company founded by Aam Anusorn. Known for its bold, heartfelt storytelling, Commetive By Aam produces films, series, and books that explore themes of identity, love, and personal growth. With a dedication to inspiring audiences to embrace their authentic selves, Commetive By Aam believes in the power of storytelling to connect, challenge, and uplift.

Commetive Read Publishing is the publishing division of Commetive By Aam, dedicated to bringing thoughtful, engaging books to readers who seek to live with purpose and self-awareness. Through insightful works like *Becoming You*, Commetive Read Publishing aims to support readers on their journey of self-discovery and growth.

Connect with Us

To stay connected, explore our projects, and join our community, you can find **Commetive By Aam** and **Aam Anusorn** on social media. Simply search **@CommetiveByAam** or **@AamAnusorn** across all platforms.

For more information, visit us online or reach out via email:

- **Website**: CommetiveByAam.com

- **Email**: info@commetivebyaam.com